READING

PRAYING IN PUBLIC

Stuart Olyott

THE BANNER OF TRUTH TRUST

THE BANNER OF TRUTH TRUST
3 Murrayfield Road, Edinburgh EH12 6EL, UK
PO Box 621, Carlisle, PA 17013, USA

*

© The Banner of Truth Trust 2008

ISBN-13: 978 0 85151 972 2

*

Typeset in 12/16 pt Adobe Garamond Pro at
The Banner of Truth Trust
Printed in the USA by
VersaPress, Inc.,
East Peoria, IL.

*

All Scripture quotations are taken from
The Holy Bible, New King James Version
Copyright © 1982 Thomas Nelson, Inc.

THE PUBLIC READING OF SCRIPTURE

So they read distinctly from the book, in the Law of God; and they gave the sense, and helped them [the hearers] to understand the reading.

Nehemiah 8:8

What you believe about the Bible, what you really believe about the Bible, comes across in the way that you read it in public. If you read it like any other book, it is because in your heart of hearts you believe that it is like any other book. Do you read it inaccurately? This is because you do not believe that every single word is important. Do you read it unattractively? This is because, in your innermost soul, you do not find the Bible captivating. Do you read it without expression? This is because you are not convinced that the Bible is a message. It is a fact that poor reading of Scripture in public reveals that the reader has problems in both his theology and his spiritual life.

So how should the Bible be read in public? We can answer this by reflecting on what we claim to believe about the Bible. There are six things to be said, some of which slightly overlap.

1. SPIRIT-INSPIRED

We believe that the Bible is Spirit-inspired. The whole book has its source in God. It is composed of books, sentences, phrases, words, and individual letters that he has 'breathed out' (*2 Tim.* 3:16). The existence of the Bible is a miracle. Without using dictation, and without destroying the individuality of each human author, God has given us a book which, in its tiniest details, is exactly what he wants it to be.

This means that the Bible has to be read for what it is – not the word of men, but the Word of God. Every time we open it, we do so in the presence of the Author. It is obvious, therefore, that nobody can read it well unless they are in living communion with God, asking for the help of his Spirit in voicing the sacred text, and praying that he will use his Word to do his work in the heart of every hearer.

2. INFALLIBLE AND INERRANT – THE VERY WORD OF GOD!

We believe that the Bible is infallible; it is entirely reliable and does not deceive us on any point. It is inerrant; it contains no mistakes. To hear it read is to hear the voice of God.

Preaching, even at its best, has error in it. But, unless it is done inaccurately, or from a faulty translation, the moment when Scripture is read is unique. No error is present. The reader speaks the Word of God. No other speech is heard. During our time on earth, this is the nearest we will get to heaven. It is, then, a moment for which both reader and hearer should prepare. This done, God's Word must be sounded out with seriousness, with reverence, and in a spirit of worship. And, because inspiration is verbal, the reader must take care how he pronounces and expresses every word.

3. PERSPICUOUS

We believe that the Bible is perspicuous. 'Perspicuous' is not a very perspicuous word, so what do we mean? We believe that the Bible is clear. This does not mean that every individual Christian understands everything that God has revealed. It is a fact, however, that the church of Jesus Christ, in every generation, is capable of understanding the heaven-given Word. This is because of the Spirit's work in the church and because of the gifts he has given to it. As far as individuals are concerned, the simplest saint is able to understand the truths that he needs to know to be saved.

It follows, then, that the Bible should be read clearly. You cannot do this if you do not understand the reading yourself. But if you do understand it, you will, inevitably, read it with expression. Some words will say to you, 'Read me high', while others will say, 'Read me low'. Some phrases will say, 'Go fast'; others will say, 'Slow down'. Certain words will declare, 'I'm loud'; others will say, 'I'm soft'. Occasional phrases will announce, 'I'm stern'; for example, 'Woe to you!' (*Matt.* 11:21). But sometimes, even in the same passage, a phrase will say, 'I'm tender'; for example, 'Come to me' (*Matt.* 11:28).

Where attention is giving to expression, the Bible will be read attractively, and the congregation will soon pick up the message that it is the most interesting book in the world. We must, however, be careful to read naturally. Listen to this paragraph from C. H. Spurgeon:

> A person who can read well is seldom met with now-a-days. The public reading of the Bible is oftentimes not worthy of being called reading. There once lived a boy in the Highlands of Scotland who presumed to read a newspaper with a twang similar to that which characterised his reading of the Bible; but his grandmother boxed the youngster's ears for presuming to read the paper in that holy way. Now, the Scriptures should be read in the best way possible – that is, naturally.

A clear reading will also have clear diction. This means that every sound of every word will be given its full value. In addition, the volume will be sufficient, so that everything is clear, even to any deaf people who may be sitting near the back. It is a mistake, however, to be satisfied with adequate volume. We need to remember that most elderly people have trouble following quick speech. For them a reading is not clear unless it is read much more slowly than normal speech.

4. FOR ALL

We believe that the Bible is for all. This being so, it needs to be read as a message for all who are present. This message is even for those who have not brought a Bible with them. If the person doing the reading looks down at the page, and those who have Bibles are doing the same, those without Bibles think to themselves, 'All this is nothing to do with me.' You have got to catch their eye! They will be surprised that you looked at them and will suddenly become aware that the reading is intended for them as well. Eye contact is an essential part of good reading. If you don't catch the eye of people without Bibles, it is probably because you do not truly believe that the reading is for them.

Maintaining eye contact during the reading is actually quite simple. If you lift the Bible off the lectern and hold it with your right hand, while following the reading with your left forefinger (something like you did as a child at school), you should have no trouble. It is now easy to look at the people in front of you, and also to find your place immediately you look down, because your finger is on the next word. Your public reading will now have much more effect and those who do not have Bibles will seldom switch off again.

5. SUPREMELY FOR THE CHURCH

We believe that the Bible, supremely, is for the church. The same manna feeds all true pilgrims and nourishes them throughout their journey from Egypt to the Promised Land. This is true in all cultures and in all generations. To change the picture, the same map is sufficient for every one of us. The same compass stops us from going off track. The same treasure chest enriches and delights every family member, whoever we are and from wherever we have come.

What a moment it is when a church of Jesus Christ gathers around the Scriptures to hear him speak! Here are the members of the body listening to their Head (*Rom.* 12:5; *Col.* 1:18). The world does not acknowledge the headship of Christ. But we do. This is a moment when headship is an important theme. This being so, it is not appropriate that a woman should do the public reading (see *1 Cor.* 11:3); nor should a child or an unconverted person. At a moment like this, not even a man should be reading in public – unless he can do it properly.

6. SUFFICIENT

Finally, we believe that the Bible is sufficient. However helpful other books may be, none of them is essential. The Bible, all on its own, is enough to bring spiritual life into existence, to sustain it and to perfect it. It does not even need anything outside of itself to prove to us that it is the Word of God. It is able to convince us of this without any additional help whatever.

What a marvellous book it is! It owes nothing to us, but we owe it everything. It stands alone. This truth is something that needs to be conveyed by the way that we read it in public. For example, it should not be read alongside any other book, because this could send the mistaken message that it is not unique. We must not even leave the impression that the Bible is the greatest book in its class.

There is one more thing to add: when we come to the end of our public reading of Scripture, we should stop and say nothing else at all. Let the Word of God ring in the silence of each listener's heart! There is a widespread habit of rounding off the reading by adding some form of pious 'ditty', as if a mortal and sinful man could somehow pronounce a blessing on the Word of God or speed it on its way. This is a bad habit and we should abandon it. Let the people be confronted with the bare Word of God! If we truly believe in the sufficiency of Scripture we will have no trouble in letting it speak for itself.

As followers of the Lord Jesus Christ we have turned our back on the desire to make a name for ourselves. This does not alter the fact that we will not be immediately forgotten after we leave this earth. If people are going to remember us, let us make sure that it is for our holy lives – and for the way that we used to read the Bible to them!

PUBLIC PRAYER

*And when he had said these things, he knelt down
and prayed with them all.*

Acts 20:36

I wonder in what contexts you lead in prayer. Do you do it in the family, at the prayer meeting, or in other formal and informal meetings of your church? I am not talking about any of those things but, rather, leading in public prayer when the whole church is gathered together in public worship.

We would all like to do this better, and we will do so if we remember four points:

1. PUBLIC PRAYER IS PUBLIC

Public and private prayer are intimately linked. A person who does not nurture and cultivate a life of private prayer, but prays like a Puritan in public, is a hypocrite – and God is against hypocrites. In our private prayer we all know that we have to 'pray until we pray'. That is not something we can do in public prayer, so we need to 'pray until we pray' in private beforehand. Then, when we come to lead in prayer in public, we will already be in the spirit of prayer.

However, although the connection between public and private prayer is intimate, we must not forget that they are distinct. Both are prayers, so both are addressed to God alone (and not to anyone who may be listening in, or to the congregation). The difference is that in private prayer I offer up my desires to God, confessing my sins, and giving thanks for the particular mercies of which I am conscious. My language is, 'I, my, me'. In public prayer my approach changes. I am now the mouthpiece of the congregation, offering up our desires to God, confessing our sins (even the ones of which I am not personally guilty), and giving thanks for the mercies of which we are conscious. My language is, 'we, our, us'.

Not only so, but private prayer, besides being spoken, may be silent; or it may simply consist of groaning. Public prayer, by definition, cannot be either of these. If it is silent, the prayer life of the church becomes a collection of voiceless private prayers. If it is groaning, it breaks the biblical rule which requires everything in the assembly to be spoken in a known tongue.

With all this in mind, a number of things become obvious. In order to be public, prayer must be audible, in a language understood by all, at a speed accessible to everyone present, in phrases that do not jar or distract, and of a length that everyone can sustain. It can only be done satisfactorily by someone who is qualified to be the mouthpiece of the congregation. This will be a person who knows the people well – their state in grace, their joys, their sorrows, their encouragements, their trials, their temptations, their needs, their preoccupations, and the events which are currently marking them and having an impact upon them.

2. PUBLIC PRAYER IS DIDACTIC

This is true whether we want it to be, or not. As we lead in prayer, we are teaching our people something. Lots of people are new in the faith. They are babes in Christ. They do not know how to pray, and they will largely take their cue from us. Our public prayers will determine the content, the manner, and the spirit of their prayers, whether those prayers be in secret, in the family, or in the prayer meeting.

If our prayers are shallow and irreverent, we will be teaching those who hear us that it is all right to be shallow and irreverent. If we fill our prayers with sickly repetitions, we will be publicly endorsing such a practice for all. If we do not pray in the Holy Spirit, nor will others, for they will never learn that there is such an experience and will have no idea what such praying is like. On the other hand, if we pray as we should, less mature believers will begin to learn to pray.

We have grossly over-estimated the prayer life of our people. Countless numbers of our brothers and sisters hardly pray at all. We can stir up their appetite. If our public prayers draw them into glory and leave them with ravished souls, they will immediately want to pray more and better.

Not only so, but there is a whole range of things which Christians should pray about; but they don't. They are a long way from exploring all the colours of the spectrum. Why is this? The reason is that they are imprisoned by the boundaries of their own thoughts. Countless subjects have never crossed their minds. If our public prayers consistently lead them into new pastures, their own prayer interests will become wider and deeper. Soon there will be much more prayer across the church for revival, for Christians in North Korea, for children with learning disabilities, for tempted ministers, for named missionaries, for lonely Bible translators, and for a whole host of other subjects.

When we lead in prayer, many people keep their eyes open. When those people see us – and everybody hears us – emotionally engaged in prayer, they will learn a great deal about Christian experience. They will eventually discern that it is the Spirit of adoption who animates our prayers, and will come into a fuller understanding of the wonder of the privileges that we have in Christ.

In addition, there are in all our congregations people who do not share our doctrinal convictions. When they see that our theology is the very pulse of our devotion, they will at last realise that it is the vision of God that has inflamed our hearts, and not a man-made system that we have coldly absorbed from heavy books. If our public prayers constantly keep in view the whole sweep of the glorious plan of redemption, they will eventually begin to grasp it, to be humbled by it, and to be thankful for it. For some of them, this bowing before the Lord will be the moment of their conversion. Our public prayers will then have proved to be not only didactic, but evangelistic.

It follows that we should be very careful about whom we call on to pray in public. Nobody should be invited except the spiritually mature. Both they and we must pray in such a way that all will have the ambition to pray well. Too many believers think that the greatest thing a Christian can do is to preach. The best way to correct this error is to pray in public in such a way that all who hear us will discern that life's greatest priority is to be in communion with God.

3. PUBLIC PRAYER SHOULD BE PASTORAL

What an important point this is! Public prayer is one of the means by which we lead people along the paths of holiness and comfort.

Let us take a moment to think about who is likely to be in the congregation. There is a discouraged Christian who is facing hostility, at school, at college, at work or in the family. There is a mother who spends long hours alone with small children. There is a businessman juggling the competing commitments of work, family, extended family, and church. There is a carer with extreme fatigue. There are elderly people for whom the next major event is death. There is the new convert, the doubter, the person going through intense or subtle temptation, the believer without assurance of salvation, and the brother or sister who is prayerfully seeking God's will. There are pastors, missionaries, Sunday-School teachers, leaders of church organisations, as well as musicians or precentors. And there are people who are ill or infirm, bereaved, redundant, suffering great loss, crushed with anxiety, or in some great need.

Each of these people finds that it is an enormous encouragement to be prayed for by the whole body to which they belong, even if they are not mentioned by name – which is our normal practice, unless we are praying for specific individuals who are ill, have had accidents, or have been bereaved. Not only so, but when any of these people are absent from public worship, they are heartened by knowing that the body of Christ is still praying for them.

Pastoral prayer does not only encourage people; it actually does something for them. The special power of congregational prayer brings blessings into people's lives. That is not all: such prayer makes those attending church sensitive to the range and weight of the needs found among their members and friends. As a result, they begin to look out for each other in a new way. They become more caring, more considerate, more patient, more willing to make allowances – and more united!

There is a further point: have you ever thought what it is like to be prayerless, backsliding, worldly, secretly nursing sin, unforgiving, and gossiping, and to hear these things prayed about in your hearing? Public prayer often prises open the locked heart, re-activates the conscience, provokes secret weeping, and woos wandering children to return to their waiting Father. It does this by being pastoral.

4. PUBLIC PRAYER MUST BE FRESH

Remaining fresh is one of the greatest challenges facing those who pray in public regularly. Prayers which are always 'the same old thing' do not glorify God; nor do they enrich those who hear them They are, in fact, damaging. They cause people to be prayerless in the very presence of prayer! The hearers groan, lose interest, switch off, and learn to tolerate a prayerless heart.

What can we do to stay fresh? We can start by preparing our prayers. I am not suggesting that we should write them down. For myself, I have found it helpful to prepare the content of the prayer, to make a few notes, but then to surrender myself to the Holy Spirit in the actual moment of praying. This ensures both fullness and variety, but also recognises that none of us can ever pray without the Lord's personal help.

We can take the time to meditate on a biblical prayer and to use it as a model. Of course, we should constantly be doing this with the Lord's Prayer. But why not sometimes do it with a psalm, or one of the other prayers recorded in the Bible, or one of the paragraphs where the apostle Paul tells us about his own prayer life?

We can discipline ourselves to regularly include every main element of prayer found in the Bible. In my understanding, there are six. They are adoration (the contemplation and worship of God), thanksgiving (for his being and his works), confession (of the sins of his people, our race, our nations, and our communities), petition (God-glorifying requests for ourselves), intercession (God-glorifying requests for others) and renewed dedication (the repeated acknowledgement that we do not belong to ourselves, but only to him who created and redeemed us).

Finally, we can encourage our prayers to take flight by making sure that they are rich in doctrine. Throughout my ministry I have found help in focusing each time on a few questions and answers of *The Shorter Catechism*,[1] and making those great truths and duties a major part of my prayer. This is effortless if you know the Catechism by heart. It encapsulates God's revelation so succinctly and fully that you feel as if your heart will burst with wonder and gratitude. Who can fail to be moved by public prayer which is driven along and given its fragrance by breezes from heaven?

---

[1] *The Westminster Shorter Catechism with Scripture Proofs* is also available from The Banner of Truth Trust as a 32 pp. pocket booklet.

Public prayer, then, is public and didactic; it should be pastoral and it must be fresh. What are people to do if they do not agree with what we have prayed on their behalf? They should remain silent and say nothing. But if they are in agreement, then, when the prayer ends, let them say loudly, and all together: Amen!

Other booklets in this series from
The Banner of Truth Trust:

For details of other helpful publications and
free illustrated catalogue please write to

THE BANNER OF TRUTH TRUST

3 Murrayfield Road,   P O Box 621, Carlisle,
Edinburgh EH12 6EL   Pennsylvania 17013,
UK   USA

www.banneroftruth.co.uk